Knightworld
The Age of Chivalry

CARLTON
BOOKS

Contents

- 6 -

Introduction

♛ ♛ ♛

- 8 -

Medieval World

- 24 -

A Knight's Realm

- 42 -

Arms and Armour

- 60 -

To Battle!

MY NAME IS HENRY TEMPLEMAN and for 40 years I have been the curator of a remote medieval castle. How the castle came to be associated with my family, I could not say, but my father performed the role before me, as did my grandfather before him. Despite my fascination with knights and castles, I would not have presumed to write a book upon the subject, were it not for a strange turn of events a few years ago...

I remember the day well, an icy morning in December when visitors to this lonely spot are but few. A couple approached me after their tour of the castle with a strange tale, for they had heard unsettling noises - urgent half-whispers around the courtyard, the pawing of hooves and muffled shouts. I did not think too much about it, but a week later, just as I was leaving for the evening, an uncanny thing occurred. It was dark by this time and I was completely alone. As I glanced into the chapel, I heard a distinct scratching noise that seemed to come from beneath the floor. Stepping in, I fancied I heard something being dragged across the floor and a muffled groan. Suddenly the door slammed shut in a freezing blast of wind and, badly frightened, I quickly hurried away. Over the next two months, several more visitors reported strange occurrences, and then the whole business seemed to die down and I almost forgot about it.

Two years later the castle required some refurbishment work. Imagine my astonishment when workers pulling up the chapel floor found a skeleton, and alongside that, a finely decorated box. Careful forensic work by specialists revealed the remains to be those of a young man in his twenties who had died some time between 1250 and 1400. Analysis of the leg bones showed they belonged to someone who had spent a lot of time on horseback, while his upper body suggested he had handled heavy weapons. There were signs of serious wounds - an arrowhead had lodged in his shoulder, while a dent to the skull was most likely caused by a severe axe blow. All the evidence showed the man had almost certainly been a mounted knight, but who was he?

AS FOR THE BOX, it was found to contain four objects: a piece of chain mail, a broken arrowhead, a bronze medallion with two figures just visible upon its dulled surface, and a rough strip of woven cloth. Although historians have dated the objects to the fourteenth century, they have been unable to identify the buried knight. In its long and turbulent history, this castle changed hands many times and was the site of several sieges. But what other mysteries, what dark plots have played out within these ancient walls?

I cannot answer these questions, but I have written this book in recognition of the man who for centuries lay forgotten beneath this castle floor: brave knight, valiant defender, or even a dark traitor perhaps? Within these pages, you will find the objects that were buried with him, shown here for the first time. And although I have presented some thoughts on each, it is right that I leave you to form your own opinions.

Henry Templeman

Medieval World

Imagine yourself alive in the year 1358.

PERHAPS YOU ARE one of the lucky few born into the top ranks of society. As a noble - a powerful lord or a valiant knight in the service of such a lord - yours is a life of privilege.

But imagine too that you are a peasant working the land, a serf with no rights or freedoms. Your master lives in a large manor house and rules over the community with an iron fist. The work is backbreaking and hunger an ever-present threat.

Here, then, is the medieval world, a place of vast contrasts ~ a world where the rich and powerful few fight to protect their position, and the many poor fight just to survive...

Rise of the Knights

FOR HUNDREDS OF YEARS, armoured knights were among the most important people in Europe and essential to success in battle. These fearsome warriors, heavily armed and trained to fight on horseback, first appeared during the eighth century in what is now France. However, they were at their most powerful from 1000 to the 1500s. During this period, mounted knights - clad in chain mail or heavy plate armour - ruled the battlefield, terrifying their enemies and pouring scorn on the common foot soldier.

The Later Middle Ages

DURING THE LATER Middle Ages - a period roughly between 1000 and 1500 - a splendid civilization developed in Europe. The chaos that followed the collapse of the Roman Empire in the fifth century had come to an end, and Europe was now more wealthy. Society was awash with new ideas, trade flourished and great castles and cathedrals were being built. However, life for most was hard. Peasants who worked the land struggled in almost constant toil, brutal wars were commonplace and disease was rife.

War and Conflict

Europe was rarely at peace in the Middle Ages. The Crusades to capture parts of the Holy Land endured for 300 years, while the Hundred Years War between France and England lasted from 1337 to 1453. Even when Europe was not at war, powerful nobles frequently carried out raids on neighbouring estates. Those lives not cut short by warfare were constantly at risk from disease.

The Black Death

Bubonic plague swept through Europe between 1346 and 1351. In just a few years, one in three people had died from this horrifying disease carried by fleas on black rats. Symptoms included a high fever and swellings on the body that turned purple-black, and oozed pus and blood. With no understanding of how diseases spread, many believed the Black Death to be a terrible punishment from God.

This scene from a medieval manuscript shows the horror of the Black Death.

Fleas carried by black rats spread the bubonic plague.

The Power of the Church

Immensely powerful, the Catholic Church was the centre of European medieval life. It owned vast amounts of land, and took a tenth of everyone's earnings in a tax called a tithe. Christians were encouraged to make pilgrimages to earn God's forgiveness, often taking long and dangerous journeys to shrines such as the tomb of St Peter in Rome. Few dared to challenge the Church's teachings; those who did were condemned, and either tortured or burned at the stake.

Medieval bishops were often rich and influential.

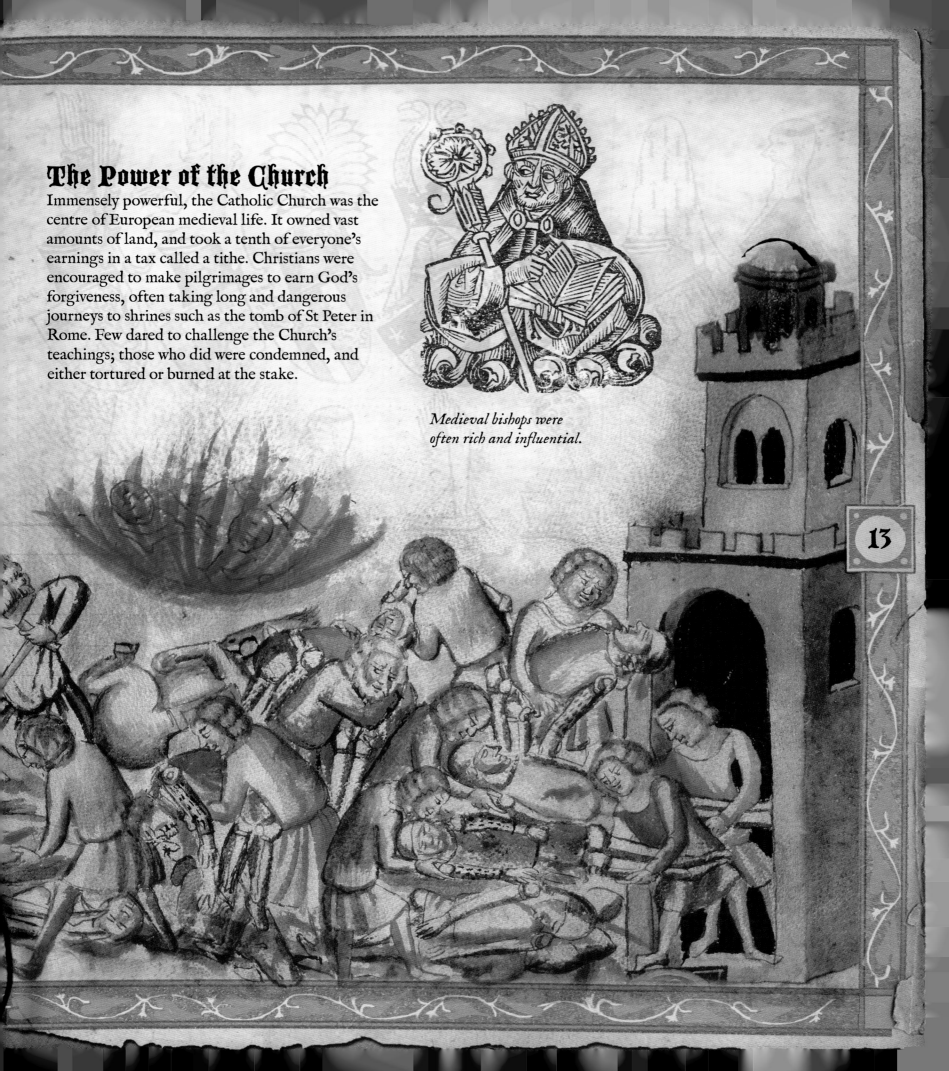

Medieval Society

I N MEDIEVAL TIMES, society was governed by a simple but effective "feudal" system, where the idea of loyalty and service was all-important. At the top of the feudal tree was the king who owned all the land in his kingdom. Beneath the monarch were his most important nobles - barons and bishops - to whom were granted large estates in return for faithful service. These powerful nobles had groups of loyal knights who provided military service in return for land. At the very bottom of the pyramid were the peasants who lived on and farmed land rented to them by the knights, thus providing food for everyone else.

The King

Medieval kings ruled by divine right, meaning it was believed that they drew their right to govern from the will of God. Although their position was beyond question, in reality a king's power was limited by his barons, upon whom he depended to provide knights in times of war. Kings often struggled to keep control of their barons, and many of these nobles grew very powerful.

Most people in medieval society were peasants who worked the land.

Barons

These rich and important nobles received land directly from the king and in return swore an oath of allegiance - "Sire, I become your man". They vowed to provide their king with knights in times of war, and to keep law and order in the areas they governed. Many barons lived in fine castles, and were given titles such as Duke or Count.

Knights

Most knights were given land and a manor house by a baron or bishop in return for loyalty and service in times of war. Bound by oath, these warriors might be called to battle at any time.

Peasants

Around 90 per cent of the people in medieval society were peasants and tied to the land they rented from the knights. According to the law, peasants could own nothing and everything they produced belonged to their lord.

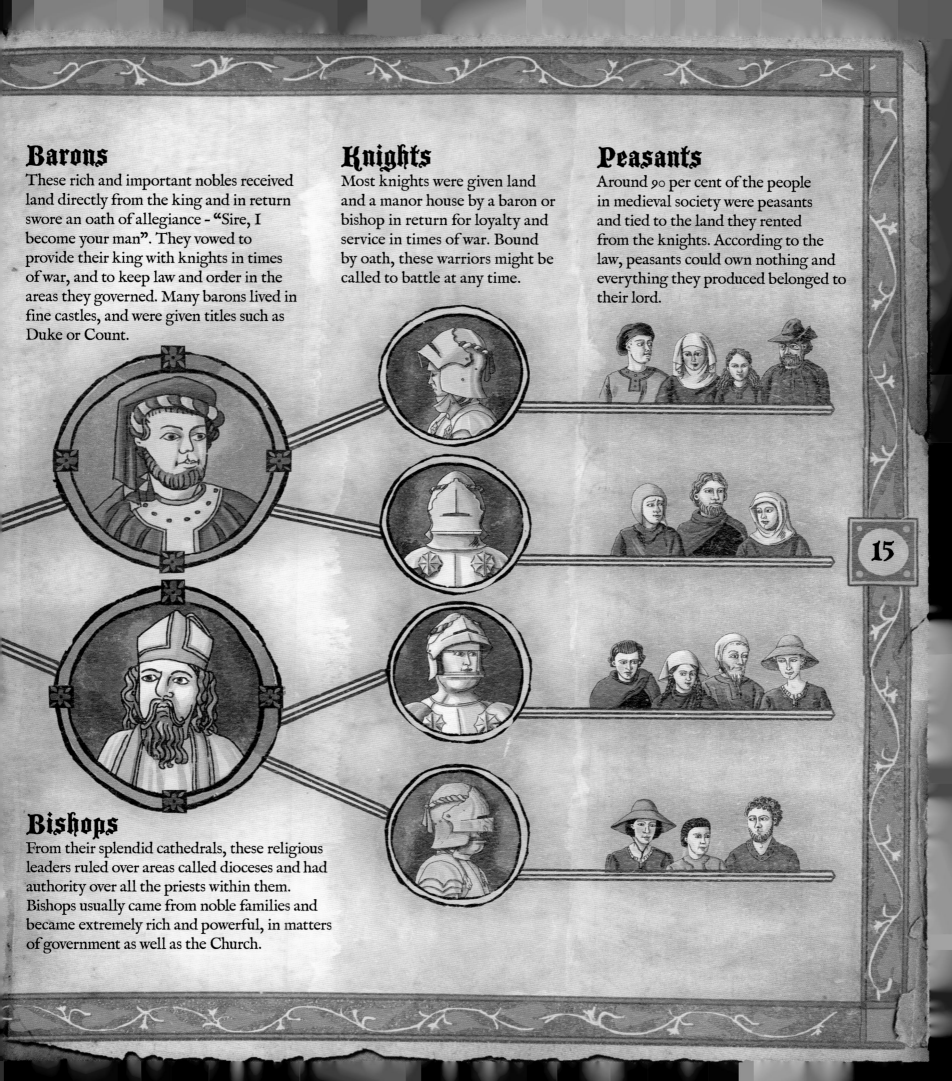

Bishops

From their splendid cathedrals, these religious leaders ruled over areas called dioceses and had authority over all the priests within them. Bishops usually came from noble families and became extremely rich and powerful, in matters of government as well as the Church.

The Castle

CASTLES DOMINATED the medieval landscape. Built to control conquered land, these fortified structures were imposing symbols of power and might. Alliances could swiftly change during the Middle Ages, and the castle was a stronghold for a baron and his supporters if they came under attack. Castles were also splendid homes to wealthy nobles, and centres for local government.

Castles in Time

€ARLY CASTLES were simple in design and constructed from local wood. However, as the need for better defences increased, wooden castles were replaced by complex stone structures that could take many years to build. Towering over the landscape, these impressive buildings dominated medieval life.

Motte and Bailey Castles

Early castles of the tenth to eleventh centuries consisted of a motte, a tall earthen mound, with a wooden tower or keep built on top (the keep was the final place of refuge should the castle's other defences be overcome). The height of the castle made it difficult to attack and easy to defend. The bailey was a fortified enclosure beneath the motte with essential buildings such as workshops and stables, as well as living quarters.

Stone Keeps

Timber castles were gradually replaced with tall stone keeps in the eleventh and twelfth centuries. Although expensive to build, these structures were much stronger and could not be burnt down. Keeps were initially square in design, but later round keeps were built, making it easier for defenders to both see and fire arrows in all directions.

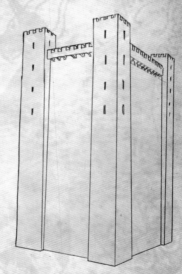

Concentric Castles

Huge concentric castles were first built in the thirteenth century. These structures had two or more rings of walls, presenting a daunting challenge to attackers. The inner walls were higher, so that archers posted here could clearly see their targets and shoot over the defenders of the outer wall. A water-filled moat often surrounded the outer castle walls, providing the first line of defence.

Castle Construction

BUILDING A STONE CASTLE was a huge undertaking, both in terms of cost and the number of years it took. Armies of skilled workers were required including stonemasons, blacksmiths and carpenters, all labouring under the direction of a master mason. The work was physically demanding and often dangerous, but the fact that so many castles remain standing today is a testament to the skill of their builders.

Hard Labour

Horse-drawn wagons were used to haul heavy stones from the quarry to the building site. Stonemasons chiselled these raw stones into blocks while blacksmiths forged nails and other fittings, and constantly sharpened the masons' tools. Meanwhile, labourers were hard at work digging ditches or mixing burnt lime with sand and water to make mortar. Treadmill cranes requiring huge muscle power were used to lift heavy blocks up to the wooden scaffolding on the castle walls. Here masons fitted the stones together with mortar and the castle gradually began to take shape.

The Castle at Peace

ALTHOUGH BUILT to defend against enemy attacks, castles were also homes to noble families and busy centres of local government. Within these fortresses, many activities took place including military training, lavish feasts and upper-class pastimes such as embroidery and chess. Behind thick, secretive walls, dark plots were hatched and important connections between noble families were built by marrying members of one to those of another.

Fit for a Lord

The great hall was where daily business was conducted and dining took place. Castles also had a large kitchen, a chapel, storerooms, workshops, stables, and a well with the vital water supply. Toilets leading to cesspits below were built into the thick walls. By modern standards, castle life would have been difficult - rooms were cold and gloomy, and there would have been little privacy for the castle's occupants.

At the High Table

Feasting was an important part of medieval life and a means of lifting spirits. The lord sat at the "high" table on a raised platform with guests seated around him in order of importance. A variety of fish and meat dishes, such as venison served with a spiced porridge called "frumenty", were served as a first course. Many courses followed and long tables were laden with meats, stuffed birds and pastries. An elaborate dish might consist of a roasted swan or peacock dressed in its feathers. People ate with their hands, sharing bowls of food and eating off slabs of stale bread called trenchers. While the diners feasted, musicians, minstrels and jesters provided entertainment.

A Knight's Realm

**Picture yourself as
a 21-year-old squire in the year 1398.**

THE OCCASION is a ceremony of knighthood, and after training in the ways of chivalry since boyhood, you are ready to enter its ranks. Your head feels light, for you have spent the night fasting and praying in the castle chapel. Robed in white, you kneel before your father as the gathered nobility look on. Your heart beats hard, for this is a moment you have long imagined and the honour is great.

Raising his sword, your father taps you on both shoulders with the blade:

"Go, fair son!
Be thou a valiant knight, and
courageous in the face of your enemies.
And be thou true and upright,
that God may love thee."

The Path to Knighthood

BECOMING A KNIGHT was not just a matter of learning to ride and handle weapons - those destined for knighthood were expected to develop a certain character. Knights were required to be loyal and fearless fighters, honourable subjects and courteous to all, especially women. Boys began their knightly training as young as seven, and typically were knighted around the age of 21.

Squires practised acrobatics to develop their strength and fitness.

From Page to Squire

A boy of noble birth was sent away to begin his training as a page in a lord's household. Here he was given a basic education, taught polite manners and how to serve at table. At the age of about 14, the page was apprenticed to a knight and served him as a squire. He learnt how to fight on horseback, looked after his master's weapons and armour, and was expected to follow him into battle. Knights needed to be extremely fit, and squires trained constantly to develop their physique and hone their fighting skills. They ran in heavy armour, practised hitting targets called quintains with a lance, and staged mock fights with each other using wooden swords and shields.

The quintain was used in training to develop accuracy with a lance.

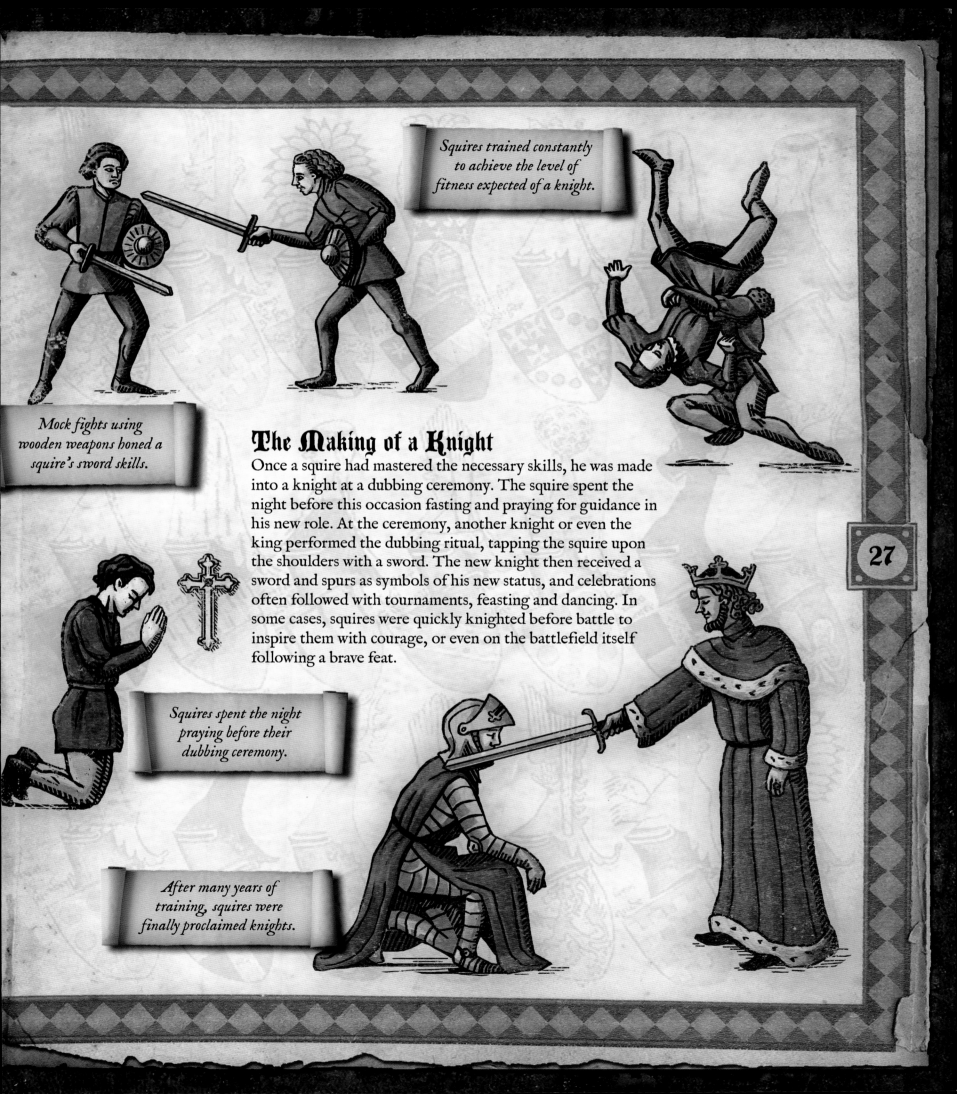

Squires trained constantly to achieve the level of fitness expected of a knight.

Mock fights using wooden weapons honed a squire's sword skills.

The Making of a Knight

Once a squire had mastered the necessary skills, he was made into a knight at a dubbing ceremony. The squire spent the night before this occasion fasting and praying for guidance in his new role. At the ceremony, another knight or even the king performed the dubbing ritual, tapping the squire upon the shoulders with a sword. The new knight then received a sword and spurs as symbols of his new status, and celebrations often followed with tournaments, feasting and dancing. In some cases, squires were quickly knighted before battle to inspire them with courage, or even on the battlefield itself following a brave feat.

Squires spent the night praying before their dubbing ceremony.

After many years of training, squires were finally proclaimed knights.

Bertrand du Guesclin

THE MOST FAMOUS French warrior of his age, Bertrand du Guesclin was an outstanding soldier and leader of men. Known as the Eagle of Brittany, he was much famed for his "hit and run" tactics that greatly weakened the English position in France during the Hundred Years War.

Small in stature and noted for being particularly ugly, he was nevertheless celebrated for his bravery and brilliance on the battlefield. Although of lowly birth, he was eventually rewarded with the highest office that his country could bestow, becoming Constable of France in 1370.

Mystery Knight

Bertrand du Guesclin was born in Dinan, Brittany around the year 1320. At the age of 17 he went to Rennes where a tournament was being held to honour the marriage of Charles de Blois. Arriving on a cart horse, he was mocked by the wealthy young knights at the contest. However, when the jousting commenced, du Guesclin borrowed a horse and secretly entered the competition. His face concealed behind his helmet, the young man proceeded to win every joust he was challenged to, felling 15 adversaries. Finally, a knight lifted the victor's visor with the tip of his lance. With the boy's identity revealed, the delighted crowd cheered while his astonished father gasped with pride.

A Fearless Fighter

Knighted in 1354, du Guesclin was to prove himself a bold and loyal warrior. In 1357, the English lieutenant Henry of Lancaster laid siege to the town of Dinan. When du Guesclin's younger brother Olivier was captured, the furious Bertrand challenged Olivier's captor - Thomas of Canterbury - to single combat. The duel began and the two mounted knights charged at one another, their lances shattering on each other's shields. After a prolonged sword fight, Thomas lost his weapon and du Guesclin swiftly dismounted to throw it out of reach. Unarmed, Thomas attempted to trample his rival beneath his horse's hooves but du Guesclin drove his sword into the animal's side, and the Englishman was thrown to the ground. The French knight dragged Thomas's helmet from his head and thrust an iron fist into his face. Victory was his.

The COAT of ARMS of
Bertrand du Guesclin

Honoured in Death

♔ ♔ ♔

OVER 23 YEARS, Bertrand du Guesclin
became one of the most successful military
generals of his time, inspiring his men with
his prowess and extreme courage. He died
in 1380 of an illness while on a military
expedition and is buried among kings
in the Abbey of St Denis in Paris -
a rare honour indeed.

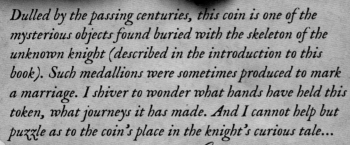

The Age of Chivalry

Dulled by the passing centuries, this coin is one of the mysterious objects found buried with the skeleton of the unknown knight (described in the introduction to this book). Such medallions were sometimes produced to mark a marriage. I shiver to wonder what hands have held this token, what journeys it has made. And I cannot help but puzzle as to the coin's place in the knight's curious tale...

Henry Templeman

KNIGHTS ACROSS Europe were bound together by a system of behaviour with strict rules and customs. This ideal of knightly conduct required that knights were brave on the battlefield, generous in victory, and courteous and honourable in their dealings with all. Although knights sometimes fell short of this ideal, to live like this was to follow the way of chivalry.

Legends and Storytelling

Stories of chivalry and heroic deeds were very popular in medieval times. In the early Middle Ages, *chansons de geste* – "songs of heroic deeds" – told of valiant heroes, cowardly traitors and beautiful princesses. Later, medieval poets called troubadours celebrated the idea of romantic love between knights and their ladies in poems and songs. The legend of King Arthur, a warrior who may have lived in the fifth century, and his Knights of the Round Table became very popular in thirteenth-century storytelling. Tales of Arthur's struggle against evil were full of adventure, romance and heroism, and strengthened medieval ideas of chivalry.

This 1900 painting by Edmund Blair Leighton shows how the idea of chivalry and courtly love has been celebrated through the ages.

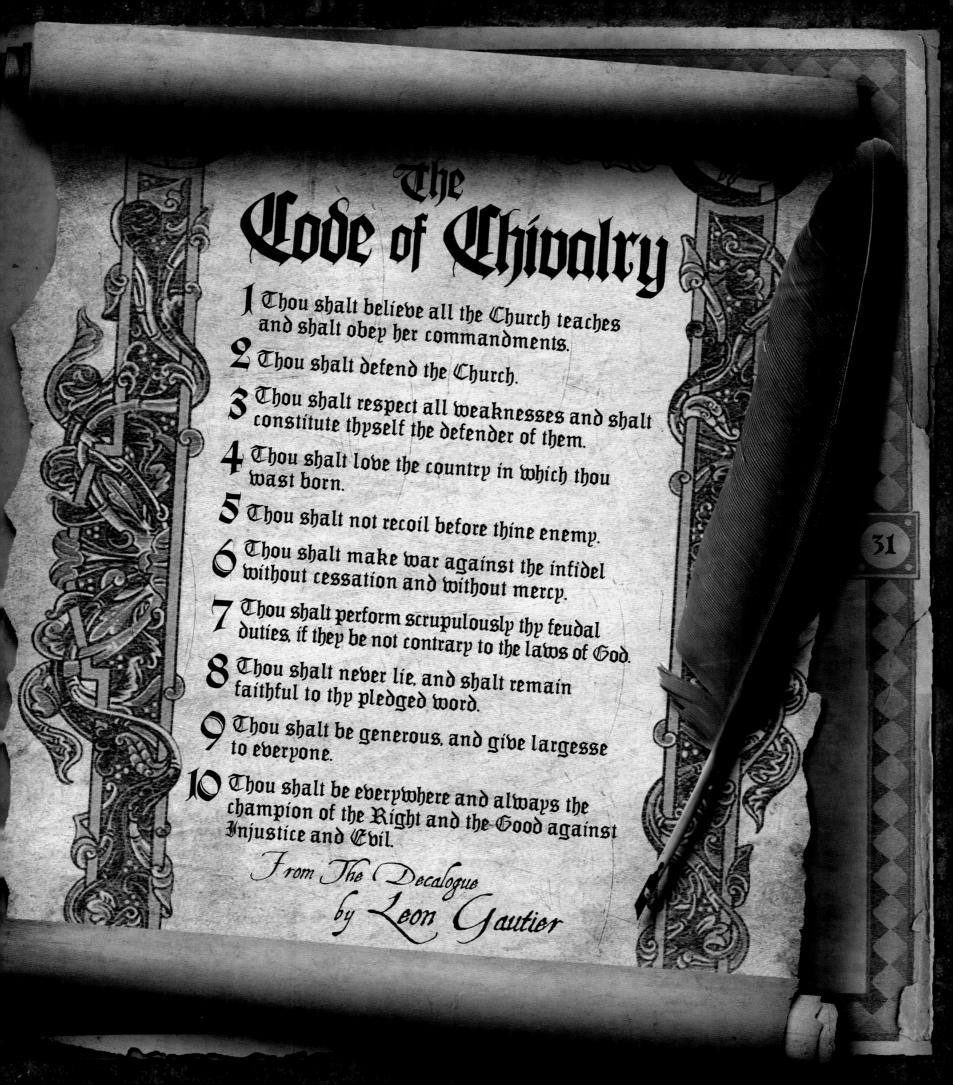

The
Code of Chivalry

1 Thou shalt believe all the Church teaches and shalt obey her commandments.

2 Thou shalt defend the Church.

3 Thou shalt respect all weaknesses and shalt constitute thyself the defender of them.

4 Thou shalt love the country in which thou wast born.

5 Thou shalt not recoil before thine enemy.

6 Thou shalt make war against the infidel without cessation and without mercy.

7 Thou shalt perform scrupulously thy feudal duties, if they be not contrary to the laws of God.

8 Thou shalt never lie, and shalt remain faithful to thy pledged word.

9 Thou shalt be generous, and give largesse to everyone.

10 Thou shalt be everywhere and always the champion of the Right and the Good against Injustice and Evil.

From The Decalogue
by Leon Gautier

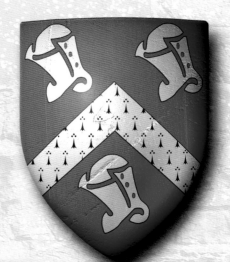

The COAT of ARMS of
Owen Tudor

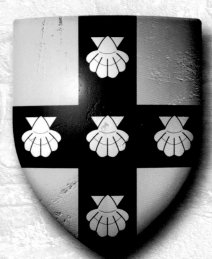

The COAT of ARMS of
Jean de Grailly

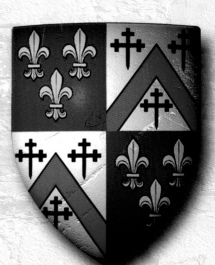

The COAT of ARMS of
Sir Hugh Kennedy

The COAT of ARMS of
Edmund Crouchback

The COAT of ARMS of
Étienne de Vignolles

The COAT of ARMS of
Pierre de Craon

The COAT of ARMS of
Prince of Gwynedd

The COAT of ARMS of
Waleran III

The COAT of ARMS of
Arther III de Bretagne

The COAT of ARMS of
Simon de Montfort

The COAT of ARMS of
Gilles de Rais

The COAT of ARMS of
Ralph de Stafford

Heraldry

At tournaments and on the battlefield, colourful patterns known as coats of arms fluttered on flags and were emblazoned on shields.

THESE SYMBOLS were a means for knights, encased in their armour, to tell friend from foe. However, they also encouraged knights to behave valiantly, for brave warriors could be easily identified, bringing glory to their families. Each noble family had its own coat of arms made up of different patterns, colours and emblems. Coats of arms were passed on from father to son, and the arms of two noble families might be combined to make a new one through marriage. The complicated job of keeping track of and recognizing the many different arms fell to trained men called heralds, and in time the system came to be known as heraldry.

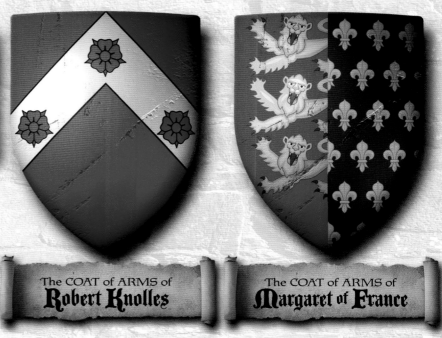

The COAT of ARMS of
Robert Knolles

The COAT of ARMS of
Margaret of France

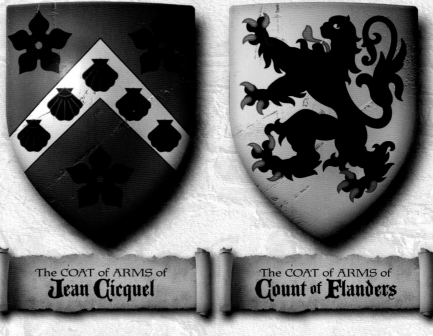

The COAT of ARMS of
Jean Cicquel

The COAT of ARMS of
Count of Flanders

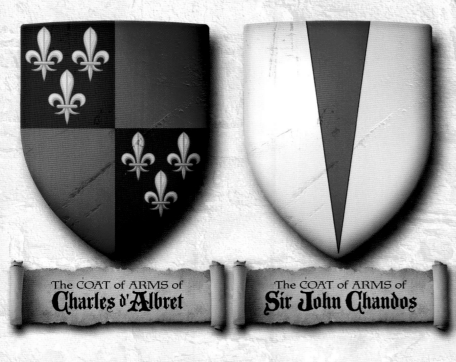

The COAT of ARMS of
Charles d'Albret

The COAT of ARMS of
Sir John Chandos

The COAT of ARMS of
Thomas de Beauchamp

The COAT of ARMS of
Thomas Blair

Hunting and Hawking

Hunting WAS a favourite pastime of medieval nobles. Large animals such as deer and wild boar were hunted on horseback, while smaller animals such as rabbits were captured using specially trained birds of prey. The sport was much more than a means of providing fresh meat for the table; it provided knights with vital training for war, and allowed rich nobles to show off their wealth and status.

The Thrill of the Hunt

Hunting on horseback was an exciting and sometimes dangerous pastime. Vast areas of forest were set aside especially for the sport - only nobles could hunt on this land and any peasants caught poaching were severely punished. Hunting dogs were used to track down animals, and sometimes peasant "beaters" were paid to run ahead and frighten animals out of their hiding places. The crossbow was a popular hunting weapon as it could be used on horseback and quickly reloaded. Dangerous tusked boars and even bears might be hunted with spears, which could be thrust into a charging animal.

The Sport of Kings

Hawking or falconry was known as the "sport of kings" as it was so expensive. Indeed, the German emperor Frederick II was so passionate about this pastime that he wrote a famous book on the subject in the mid-thirteenth century. Wild birds of prey were caught when they were very young and trained to capture and kill animals without eating them. The rarest hunting birds - eagles, gyrfalcons and peregrine falcons - were reserved for kings and the highest-ranking nobles, while people from the lower ranks of nobility hunted with less valuable birds such as sparrowhawks.

Hunting horns were used
to communicate with other
hunters, and to send signals
to hunting dogs.

Tournaments

This strip of cloth appears to have been torn from a knight's surcoat, though it has not been possible to identify the coat of arms. One can make out the fleur-de-lis, a heraldic symbol long associated with French kings, and used on countless European coats of arms from the twelfth century. It is easy to suppose this fragment was part of the buried knight's arms, proudly displayed in battle and emblazoned on his shield at tournaments.

Henry Templeman

THROUGHOUT HISTORY warriors have always trained for war, and tournaments were at the centre of knightly life. In carnival-like events that could last for several days, individuals and teams of men fought each other in mock battles. These military games kept knights fit and were a chance for them to show off their fighting skills. Tournaments were highly popular with spectators but frowned upon by the Church, for injury and death were not uncommon. In one tournament held in Neuss, France in 1240, 60 knights died, many of them suffocated by heat beneath their armour.

This jousting helm allowed a knight to see his opponent when crouching forward, but still protected his eyes.

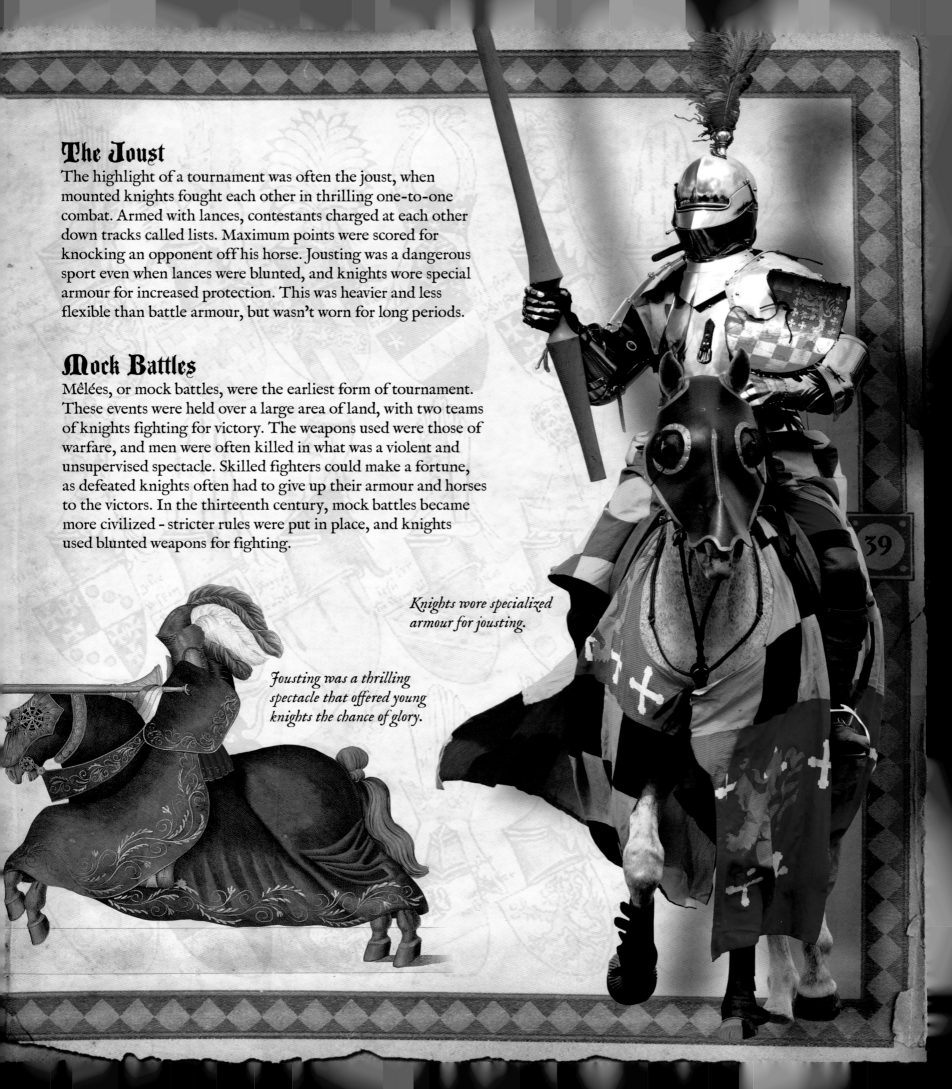

The Joust

The highlight of a tournament was often the joust, when mounted knights fought each other in thrilling one-to-one combat. Armed with lances, contestants charged at each other down tracks called lists. Maximum points were scored for knocking an opponent off his horse. Jousting was a dangerous sport even when lances were blunted, and knights wore special armour for increased protection. This was heavier and less flexible than battle armour, but wasn't worn for long periods.

Mock Battles

Mêlées, or mock battles, were the earliest form of tournament. These events were held over a large area of land, with two teams of knights fighting for victory. The weapons used were those of warfare, and men were often killed in what was a violent and unsupervised spectacle. Skilled fighters could make a fortune, as defeated knights often had to give up their armour and horses to the victors. In the thirteenth century, mock battles became more civilized - stricter rules were put in place, and knights used blunted weapons for fighting.

Knights wore specialized armour for jousting.

Jousting was a thrilling spectacle that offered young knights the chance of glory.

39

Arms and Armour

Imagine you are a knight preparing for battle in the late thirteenth century.

GROUPED IN CLOSELY KNIT ROWS, you and 100 fellow horsemen are sweltering beneath heavy armour, the metal tips of your lances glinting in the hot sun. Through the narrow slits of your helmet you survey the scene, observing the enemy gathered in the distance. Horses restlessly paw the ground and the air is heavy with tension.

An order comes for the charge. With horses evenly spaced, you push your mounts into a steady trot. Then as your enemy comes within striking distance, lances are levelled and horses spurred into a furious gallop. The air is filled with the thud of hooves, the splintering of wood, the clash of metal, the agonized cries of men and horses.

As you break through the ranks of foot soldiers, swords are drawn and close-quarter combat begins...

Suits of Iron

IF A KNIGHT was to survive a battle, his body needed to be shielded from swords, arrows and other deadly weapons. Early knights wore tunics of chain mail - armour consisting of small interlocking iron rings. During the fourteenth century, knights began to add steel plates for extra protection, and by the fifteenth century these warriors were wearing full suits of plate armour.

Chain Mail

The hauberk - a long chain mail shirt reaching to the knees - was the chief feature of early medieval armour. Making chain mail was both expensive and time consuming - several thousand iron rings were needed for just one tunic, and had to be individually linked together. This armour was flexible, but could still be pierced by arrows and so knights wore padded vests called aketons to absorb heavy blows. During the twelfth century, hauberk sleeves became longer, and leggings were also worn, made either from chain mail or leather. Early knights carried large wooden shields and wore helmets, perhaps with a bar to shield the nose, as well as mail hoods.

This fragment of rusted chain mail lay concealed beneath a castle floor for close to 800 years. Perhaps it belonged to the mysterious knight, cut from his body in death. Or was it a trophy from some long-forgotten contest, plucked from the battlefield in victory?

Henry Templeman

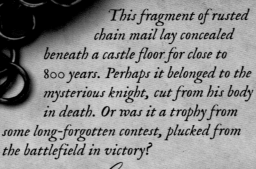

An armourer links iron rings together to make a hauberk.

A replica of a Norman helmet. The nasal bar protected the wearer's nose.

Plate Armour

AS MEDIEVAL WEAPONS grew ever more deadly, armour became increasingly elaborate. By the end of the Middle Ages, knights were wearing full body armour made almost entirely from overlapping steel plates. Despite appearances, plate armour was actually more comfortable than chain mail as the weight was spread evenly over the body. A suit might weigh up to 25 kg, but although a knight would need help arming for the fight, once dressed in his armour he could run or mount his horse unaided.

Flexible Joints

A suit of plate armour was made by highly skilled craftsmen and extremely expensive. The steel plates needed to be designed in such a way that they moved with the man wearing the armour. Rich knights could buy high-quality armour assembled from parts that were specially crafted to fit their bodies. Armour that imitated fashionable clothing was much in demand but particularly expensive. Some pieces were engraved, others featured stylish "pleats", and gold plating was sometimes used as decoration.

A full suit of plate armour allowed a knight to move freely, but the wearer quickly became very hot.

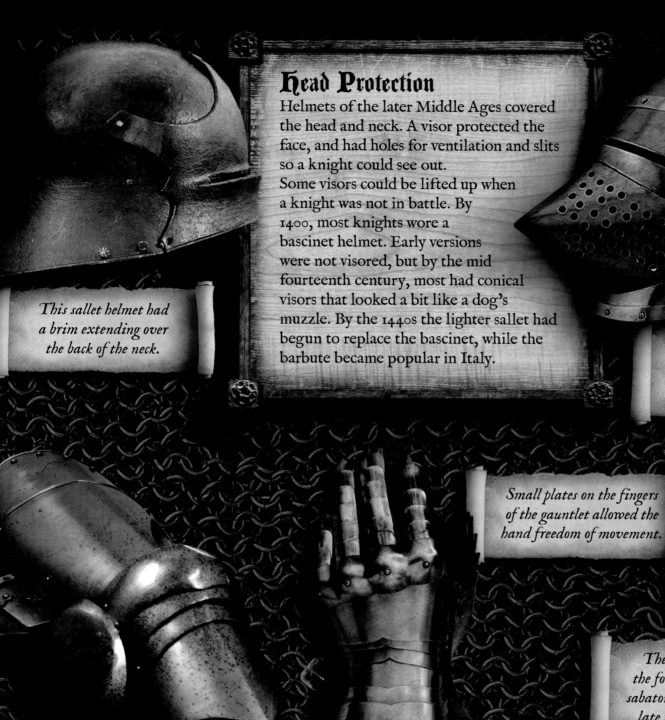

Head Protection

Helmets of the later Middle Ages covered the head and neck. A visor protected the face, and had holes for ventilation and slits so a knight could see out.
Some visors could be lifted up when a knight was not in battle. By 1400, most knights wore a bascinet helmet. Early versions were not visored, but by the mid fourteenth century, most had conical visors that looked a bit like a dog's muzzle. By the 1440s the lighter sallet had begun to replace the bascinet, while the barbute became popular in Italy.

This sallet helmet had a brim extending over the back of the neck.

The hounskull was a type of bascinet helmet with a pointed visor that resembled a dog's muzzle.

Small plates on the fingers of the gauntlet allowed the hand freedom of movement.

The sabaton protected the foot. Slender, pointed sabatons were seen from the late fourteenth century.

The cuisse protected the thigh, while the knee guard or poleyn allowed the knee to bend freely.

Edward the Black Prince

ALTHOUGH PRINCE EDWARD, eldest son of Edward III, never became King of England, he is remembered as a great medieval hero. Bold and valiant in battle, he showed military brilliance from a very early age, achieving glory with victories against the French during the Hundred Years War. Within his lifetime he was known as Edward of Woodstock after the Oxfordshire town of his birth. The title of the Black Prince came into being after his death, and most likely refers to the black armour that he wore in battle.

Glory at the Battle of Crécy

Edward's first taste of triumph came with his father's invasion of Normandy in 1346. Aged just 16, the prince was knighted by the king, and put in charge of one of the army divisions. Thousands of French troops led by King Philip VI rushed to meet the English advance, and the two sides fought a fierce battle at the village of Crécy.

Although the English were heavily outnumbered, charging French knights were cut down by a hail of longbow arrows and were unable to penetrate English lines. However, at one point the young Edward found his troops surrounded, and a message was sent to his father for assistance. According to a court historian, the king replied, "Is my son dead, unhorsed, or so badly wounded he cannot support himself? Let the boy win his spurs!"

By midnight the battle was over. Up to 10,000 French lay dead, including many important nobles, and Prince Edward had indeed won his spurs.

The Black Prince poses heroically in both crown and armour.

The COAT of ARMS of
Edward the Black Prince

Mixed Fortunes

In 1357, Edward - now aged 26 - led the English to another stunning victory against the French at Poitiers, capturing the French king Jean II. Edward famously insisted on serving the king at dinner that evening. Five years later, Edward was created Prince of Aquitaine and took up his duties in France. In 1367 the prince led an expedition to Spain to restore King Pedro of Castile to the throne, and again was triumphant at the battle of Najera. However, the campaign made him unpopular with his nobles in Aquitaine and they soon revolted. Edward responded by besieging the town of Limoges and massacring 3,000 of its inhabitants. A year later, the Black Prince returned to England where he died in 1376. His son Richard - aged just 10 - succeeded Edward III as king a year later.

Weaponry

HIS SWORD WAS undoubtedly a knight's most treasured weapon. This symbol of knighthood itself carried prestige and honour, and was vital for close-quarter fighting. However, the medieval battlefield saw the use of many other deadly weapons, and a knight's training ensured he had mastery of them all.

Sword (below)

As medieval warfare and armour changed, so too did the sword. A double-edged slashing sword was used in battle until the late thirteenth century, but as plate armour gradually replaced chain mail, swords became smaller and more pointed. These later weapons could be thrust through gaps in an opponent's armour and helmet, causing dreadful injuries.

Lance

Mounted knights charged with lances, long wooden poles with sharp metal tips. Imagine the force of these lethal weapons as two horses approached each other at speeds of up to 95 km/h! In the fourteenth century, lances were equipped with vamplates, small round plates to stop the hand sliding up the shaft on impact.

Battle Axe

This weapon, most often used on horseback, could strike an enemy at close range. Battle axes went somewhat out of favour after 1100, but became popular again after 1400 when plate armour demanded the development of weapons with high impact. Similarly, the late medieval war hammer was able to smash through helmets and breastplates.

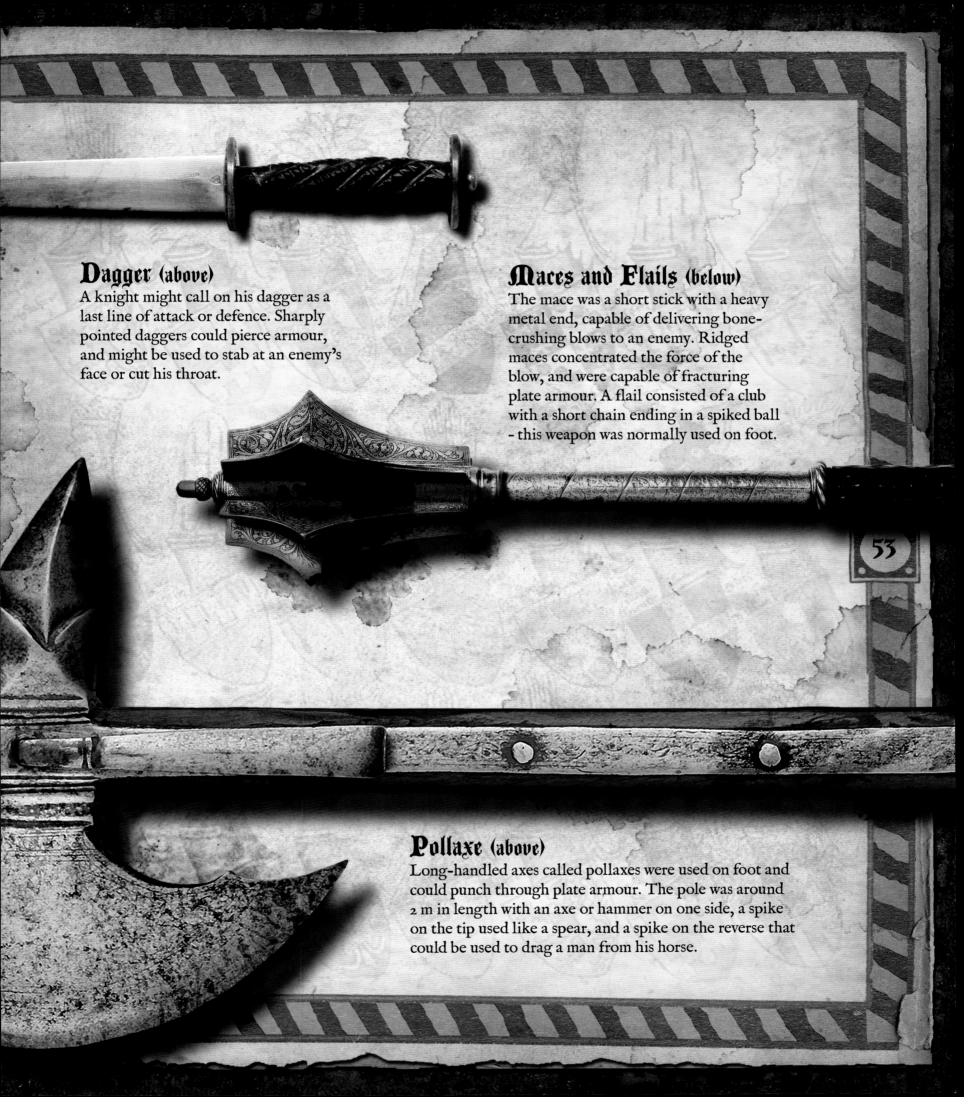

Dagger (above)

A knight might call on his dagger as a last line of attack or defence. Sharply pointed daggers could pierce armour, and might be used to stab at an enemy's face or cut his throat.

Maces and Flails (below)

The mace was a short stick with a heavy metal end, capable of delivering bone-crushing blows to an enemy. Ridged maces concentrated the force of the blow, and were capable of fracturing plate armour. A flail consisted of a club with a short chain ending in a spiked ball - this weapon was normally used on foot.

Pollaxe (above)

Long-handled axes called pollaxes were used on foot and could punch through plate armour. The pole was around 2 m in length with an axe or hammer on one side, a spike on the tip used like a spear, and a spike on the reverse that could be used to drag a man from his horse.

Cross-guard

Scabbard

Blade

Grip

Pommel

Bless with the right hand of
Thy Majesty

this Sword,

*that it may be a defence
of churches, widows, orphans
and all Thy servants.*

FROM A MEDIEVAL CEREMONY
TO BLESS A KNIGHT'S SWORD

A Knight's Horses

APART FROM HIS ARMOUR and sword, a knight's most valued possession was surely his warhorse or "destrier". Knights trusted their mounts to be nimble in the charge, and to fearlessly plunge into the violent confusion of battle. Many knights had two or more warhorses, as well as several other horses with different uses. When travelling, a knight usually rode a horse called a palfrey, while a packhorse known as a sumpter horse was used for carrying baggage.

Spurs, attached to the heel and used to urge a horse on, were an important emblem of knighthood.

Armed for the Fight

Horse armour was very expensive and not commonly used. If a knight could only afford one piece, he would choose the shaffron which protected the horse's face. Warhorses were very vulnerable to being stabbed in the belly during battle, and were trained to twist and trample when surrounded by foot soldiers.

Charging French knights are thrown from their horses as they stumble over a ditch at the Battle of Courtrai in 1302.

A knight's warhorse needed the following qualities:

"a man's boldness, a woman's movement, a fox's trot, a hare's eyes and an ass's strong legs"

<small>FROM A FIFTEENTH-CENTURY TEXT</small>

A knight and his steed, ready for battle. Only the wealthiest knights could afford armour for their horses.

57

To Battle!

The year is 1324 and your lord has gathered all his knights in a hostile attack against the castle of a neighbouring shire.

NOBODY HAS LEFT or entered the castle for two long months and your army has blocked all news of the outside world. Food and water are now scarce for the castle occupants, who have begun eating rats to survive. Indeed, the castle has become their prison rather than their protector.

Daily bombardments cause terror as rocks shatter against the walls from all sides. Hidden behind these walls, enemy crossbowmen survey your comrades and their horses, carefully aiming bolts through slit-like windows. In turn, you hurl human body parts and other missiles into the castle, hoping to create an unbearable stench. Striding up to the gatehouse, a messenger brings the captives grim tidings:

**"Surrender now,
or torture and a terrible
death await all..."**

The Crusades

THE CRUSADES were a series of holy wars fought by Christians against Muslims to capture parts of the Holy Land. As the place of Christ's birth and death, Jerusalem was very important to Christians. However, in the late eleventh century, new Muslim rulers - Seljuk Turks - came to power and made it much harder for Christian pilgrims to visit the city. In 1095, Pope Urban II called upon all Christian kings to send their warriors to the Holy Land and liberate it.

Pope Urban II called upon Christian countries to march to the defence of the Holy Land with the words, "Let none hesitate... God wills it!"

NORTH SEA

ENGLAND

BOHEMIA

ATLANTIC OCEAN

GERMANY

FRANCE

PORTUGAL

ARAGON

ITALY

CASTILE

GRANADA

MOROCCO

Crusaders set sail for the Holy Land across the Mediterranean Sea.

"God Wills It!"

This was the battle cry of the 30,000 knights and soldiers who answered the pope's plea, and made the long and dangerous journey across Europe to the Holy Land. Travelling both overland and by sea, it took the knights and soldiers up to 11 months to reach their destination. This First Crusade was a success for the huge Christian army, and Jerusalem and other cities fell to the invaders. However, in 1187, the Muslims recaptured Jerusalem under their great leader Saladin. Over the next 200 years, there were seven further crusades and much bloodshed, but the Christians never reclaimed Jerusalem.

The great Muslim leader Saladin was admired for his bravery on the battlefield and for his noble character.

The ancient city of Jerusalem was captured by the Crusaders in 1099, but fell once again to the Muslims in 1187.

N

W

E

S

RUSSIA

POLAND

HUNGARY

BULGARIA

SERBIA

BYZANTINE EMPIRE

BLACK SEA

ASIA MINOR

Manzikert

Antioch

HOLY LAND

MEDITERRANEAN SEA

Jerusalem

EGYPT

Key

Christian territories	Crusaders' routes to the Holy Land
Muslim territories	Battles

Crusader Kings

Frederick I Barbarossa

THE NAME of the German warrior king Frederick I Barbarossa was known throughout Europe. Crowned Emperor of the Holy Roman Empire in 1155, it was Barbarossa's dream to restore Germany to the that glory she had enjoyed under the eighth-century Frankish leader Charlemagne. As a result, this warrior king's life was full of feuds, dark intrigue and brutal wars with the cities of northern Italy.

Death of the King

By the end of 1187, Jerusalem was once again under Muslim control, and Pope Gregory VIII immediately called upon Europe's kings to lead a new crusade to the Holy Land. Skilled in arms and a great military leader, Barbarossa was an old man when he led a huge German army of 100,000 men on the Third Crusade in 1189. He reached Asia Minor, but while trying to cross a river, his horse was swept away by a swift current and the emperor drowned.

Legendary Warrior

A legend sprung up around the much-loved Barbarossa that he was not really dead, but asleep in a cave among the German Kyffhäuser hills, surrounded by gallant knights. It was said that when the ravens ceased to fly around the mountains, then this mighty warrior would awake and come once more to rule over Germany.

Richard the Lionheart

NOBLE, FIERCE and courageous, Richard I of England was one of the great warrior kings of the Middle Ages. Displaying military brilliance from an early age, his heroic exploits during the Third Crusade earned him the name "Lionheart". Never happier than when engaged in battle, Richard was first and foremost a soldier, and in fact spent only a few months of his 10-year reign in England.

Taking up the Cross

Once Richard had become king in 1189, he immediately began raising funds for the Third Crusade and set sail for the Holy Land in 1190. Joining the French king Philip II at the siege of Acre in 1191, Richard breathed new life into the crusader army, and the town fell within a month. Despite further important victories, Richard soon came to realize that even if he could capture Jerusalem, he would not be able to defend it.

In 1192, the king turned back. However, in Vienna he was captured by Duke Leopold of Austria - with whom he had quarrelled at Acre - and was handed over to the German emperor Henry VI, who held Richard prisoner until a huge ransom could be paid in 1194. The English king's final years were spent at war with Philip II of France, and in 1199 he was mortally wounded while besieging the French town of Chalus. Chivalrous to the last, it is said that upon his deathbed, he granted the crossbowman who had injured him a pardon.

The COAT of ARMs of
Richard the Lionheart

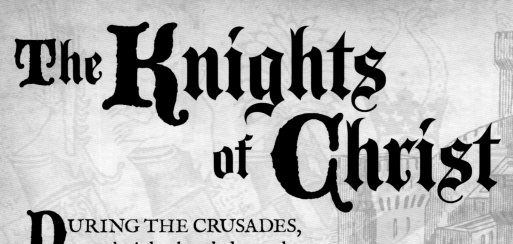

The Knights of Christ

DURING THE CRUSADES, some knights banded together and formed religious orders of monks. The Knights Templar was founded in Jerusalem in 1118 to protect pilgrims visiting the Holy Land. Like other monks, members swore vows of chastity and poverty, but they were warriors too, prepared to die for their faith. Another order of warrior monks known as the Knights of St John (or the Hospitallers) cared for sick Christians, as did the German Teutonic Knights, an order formed during the Third Crusade. These orders grew to become immensely wealthy, building magnificent castles including the Hospitaller stronghold Krac des Chevaliers.

66

Templar knights, in their distinctive white surcoats with a red cross, were amongst the most skilled fighters of the Crusades.

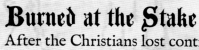

The Knights Hospitaller

The Teutonic Knights

Burned at the Stake

After the Christians lost control of the Holy Land in 1291, support for the Knights Templar began to fade. The French king Philip IV, deeply in debt to the order, had many of its members in France arrested for witchcraft, tortured and burned at the stake. The order was disbanded in 1312. The Hospitallers moved to Rhodes and then Malta in the Mediterranean, where its knights continued the fight against the Muslims. The Teutonic Knights moved its base to eastern Europe, fighting violent crusades against pagans.

67

As well as fighting for their faith, both the Knights Hospitaller (left) and the Teutonic Knights (right) looked after sick and injured pilgrims visiting the Holy Land.

Dating from the period of the Crusades, the two sides of this rare coin discovered in Jaffa, Israel show Christian symbols. The Knights Templar, the Knights Hospitaller and the Teutonic Knights all became very wealthy.

Under Siege

CAPTURING CASTLES was a crucial part of medieval warfare. However, most castles were very well defended and taking control of them was no easy task. An attacking army might surround a castle, cutting off all food supplies and wait for the starving occupants to surrender - a process that could take several months. The quicker option was a full-scale attack, where soldiers would get through the castle walls by breaking them down or climbing over them.

Breaching the Walls

Attacking soldiers used a range of tactics and equipment to overcome a castle's defences. Tunnels might be dug under the castle foundations; these could then be collapsed to bring down the walls above. Huge weapons called siege engines were used to crash through the castle walls, battering rams could be rammed against the gate to smash it down, and trebuchets used to catapult heavy rocks and boulders. Other missiles such as dead animals, manure or flaming "firepots" might also be launched over the walls. Ballistas were giant crossbows that could fire huge arrows at enemy soldiers, and from the 1300s cannons were used to fire stone and iron balls. Tall wooden siege towers allowed soldiers to climb over the battlements, or the men might quickly ascend the walls with scaling ladders.

The siege tower protected both knights and ladders when approaching a castles' battlements.

The trebuchet was essentially a giant catapult, used to hurl massive boulders at solid castle walls.

Like a enormous crossbow, the ballista fired huge, iron-clad arrows with extreme force.

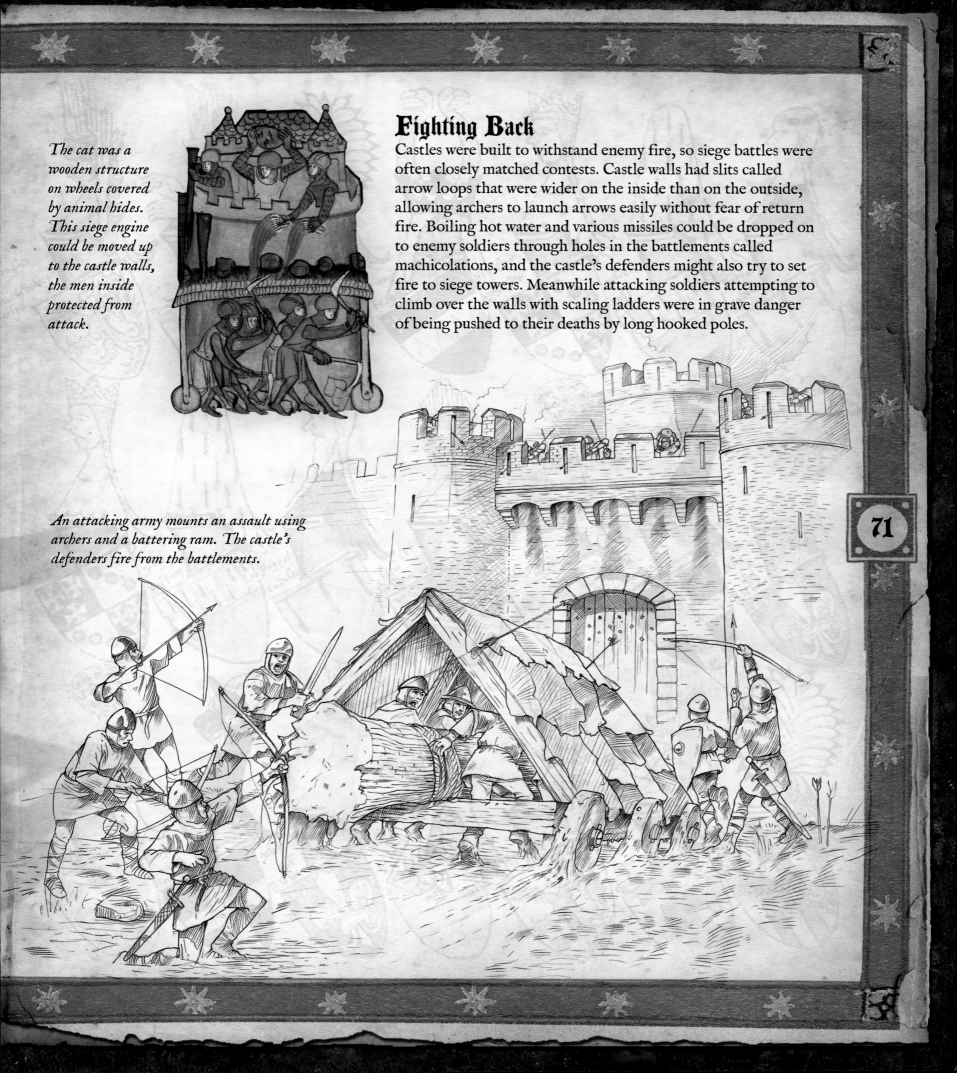

The cat was a wooden structure on wheels covered by animal hides. This siege engine could be moved up to the castle walls, the men inside protected from attack.

Fighting Back

Castles were built to withstand enemy fire, so siege battles were often closely matched contests. Castle walls had slits called arrow loops that were wider on the inside than on the outside, allowing archers to launch arrows easily without fear of return fire. Boiling hot water and various missiles could be dropped on to enemy soldiers through holes in the battlements called machicolations, and the castle's defenders might also try to set fire to siege towers. Meanwhile attacking soldiers attempting to climb over the walls with scaling ladders were in grave danger of being pushed to their deaths by long hooked poles.

An attacking army mounts an assault using archers and a battering ram. The castle's defenders fire from the battlements.

71

Enemy Foot Soldiers

ALTHOUGH KNIGHTS were the dominant force on the medieval battlefield, they increasingly faced an enemy capable of defeating them. In 1302, poorly trained Flemish foot soldiers armed with clubs shockingly defeated an army of French knights at Courtrai, while Scottish soldiers held off English cavalry charges with their spears at the Battle of Bannockburn in 1314. The face of medieval warfare was perhaps changed forever in 1346 when the best of French knighthood was cut down by a storm of English longbow arrows at the Battle of Crécy.

Arrow Storm!

The longbow was not a new weapon, but in the thirteenth century the English adopted a devastating tactic. By grouping thousands of archers together, a hail of arrows could be sent hissing down on enemy knights, creating a lethal firepower. Skill was required to use the longbow effectively, but once trained an archer could shoot up to 10 arrows a minute to hit a target up to 250 m away. Horses were particularly vulnerable to this form of attack, and the animals became extremely difficult to control when wounded.

The Powerful Crossbow

A popular weapon on the European mainland, the crossbow became an increasingly dangerous threat on the battlefield. Crossbowmen required less training than longbowmen, and although the weapon could only shoot two metal bolts in a minute, these deadly missiles were capable of punching through a knight's armour.

Easier to use than the longbow, the powerful crossbow posed a dangerous threat to knights.

Thousands of French knights were cut down by longbow arrows at the Battle of Crécy in 1346.

The longbow shot a range of specialized arrows, from flesh-piercing broadheads to bodkins that could punch through armour.

Spears and Pikes

Foot soldiers brandishing long spears or pikes and grouped in close formation could prove a lethal threat to mounted knights. Just such a danger lay in wait when the Scottish king and hardened warrior Robert the Bruce faced the English king Edward II at the Battle of Bannockburn. The Scots army were outnumbered nearly three to one, but on this occasion the sheer numbers of the English cavalry proved to be their own downfall. Facing a bristling forest of Scottish spears, the English were forced back. Mounted knights struggled to retreat on the boggy land, and fallen men were trampled underfoot.

Pikemen, grouped in close formation, could effectively hold off a cavalry charge.

The 100 Years War

KING CHARLES IV of France died in 1328 without leaving an heir, and his grandson Edward III of England made a claim to the French throne. So began a series of battles fought between French and English kings known as the Hundred Years War. At first the superior battle tactics of the English brought them a number of victories, notably at the battles of Crécy, Poitiers and Agincourt. However, with the appearance of Joan of Arc in 1429, French fortunes dramatically changed, and the war finally ended in 1453 with the French king Charles VII driving the English almost completely out of France.

The Battle of Agincourt

When Henry V became king of England in 1413, he immediately renewed Edward III's claim to the French throne. In October 1415, after a series of campaigns, a French army of up to 30,000 knights faced 6,000 archers and knights led by King Henry. The battle took place in a muddy field in northern France. After waiting in vain for the French to attack, Henry marched his army close enough to unleash a hail of arrows upon them. The French mounted knights charged forward, but they were bogged down by slippery mud and crippled by the arrows raining down upon them. As the knights fled back through the advancing French footsoldiers, the English archers dropped their longbows and, picking up swords and axes, joined their comrade knights in slaying the foe.

The English use of the longbow was crucial to victory against the French at the battles of Crécy, Poitiers and Agincourt.

Edward III's English army crosses the Somme river in France prior to the Battle of Crécy.

> "We few, we happy few,
> we band of brothers;
> For he today that sheds
> his blood with me
> Shall be my brother…"

King Henry V

A RALLYING SPEECH
TO HIS MEN AT AGINCOURT,
FROM SHAKESPEARE'S "HENRY V"

Joan of Arc

By 1429, France was weak and divided, much of her land lost to the English. However, with the rise to power of Joan of Arc, a young peasant girl, French fortunes took a miraculous change of direction. At the age of 16, Joan claimed she heard voices telling her it was God's mission for her to liberate France. Given troops to command, Joan breathed new life into the French army, inspiring it to break the siege of Orléans in April 1429, and to further dramatic victories. However, just over a year later Joan was captured, tried as a witch and burnt at the stake by the English.

The COAT of ARMs of
Joan of Arc

The Last Knights

AS THE MIDDLE AGES drew to a close, knights found that they were increasingly forced to fight on foot. Even heavily armed, they were no contest for solid formations of skilled pikemen, and expensive plate armour could not protect a knight from powerful new weapons such as the arquebus, a firearm that came into use in the fifteenth century. Rulers now preferred to pay trained foot soldiers to fight their battles. Meanwhile, cannons and gunpowder became more effective, and artillery forts that could withstand heavy gunfire began to be built. There was no longer a need for castles, and while some were converted into fortresses or homes, many fell into ruin.

THE GREAT AGE of the knight was coming to an end, but its ideals of chivalry - of loyalty, honesty and courage - and thrilling tales of brave warriors and heroic deeds, live on in legends to this day.

Acknowledgements

THE SUBJECT OF KNIGHTS has long fascinated me – indeed my surname can be traced back to the time of the crusading order the Knights Templar, so-called because of their association with the site of the old temple in Jerusalem. However, I would not have thought to write upon the subject were it not for the curious turn of events outlined in my introduction. In drawing upon that inspiration, I have been assisted by many. As well as thanking my family, I would like to acknowledge the expertise of those who have guided me in the writing of this book, and the vision of those who have been instrumental in its design and production:

The consultant *Peter Chrisp*; my editor *Barry Timms*; the designers *Russell Porter* and *Clare Baggaley*; *Drew McGovern* and *Danny Baldwin* for Photoshop and design work; *Somchitch Vongprachanh* and *Andrew Kerr* for the CGI artwork: *Leo Brown* and *Rebecca Wright* for their illustrations; *Ben White* for picture research; and *Christine Ni* for production.

Henry Templeman

80

Picture Credits

The publishers would like to thank the following sources for their kind permission to reproduce the pictures in this book.

Key: T=top, L=left, R=right, C=centre, B=bottom.

AKG Images: 38, /Jérôme da Cunha: 56b, /Hermann Historica: 44br, /Joseph Martin: 62c, /North Wind Picture Archives: 57
Alamy: /Art Archive: 12-13, 74r, /Art Gallery Collection: 22-23, /Lebrecht Music and Arts Photo Library: 10-11, /The Print Collector: 56t
Bridgeman Art Library: /Ashmolean Museum, University of Oxford: 36-37, /Bibliotheque des Arts Decoratifs/Archives Charmet: 62b, 66, /British Library: 63c, 71, /Collection of the Earl of Leicester, Holkham Hall: 73t, /Look & Learn: 70r, /Philip Mould: 50r, /National Portrait Gallery: 75, /Stadtbibliothek, Nuremburg, Germany: 44bl, /The Stapleton Collection: 38-39
Corbis: /Angelo Hornak: 78-79, /Christie's Images: 30b
DK Images: 46, 52-53, 72bl
Get Dressed for Battle Ltd: 47bl
Getty Images: 67, 67r, /Dorling Kindersley: 45
Heritage Images: /The Board of the Trustees of the Armouries: 70l, / British Library: 20b
iStockphoto.com: 50l,
Knights Edge Ltd: 47bl
Paul Lantz: 64
Lebrecht Music & Arts: 63b, 66-67, /RA: 14
Joe Metz: 67l
Photo 12: /Ann Ronan Picture Library: 13t,
Royal Armouries: 47tl
Russell Porter: 1, 2-3, 8-9, 24-25, 28, 32-33, 39r, 40-41, 47bc, 48-49, 52c, 54-55, 58-59, 60-61, 73r, 74r, 76-77, 80
Scala Archives: /The Metropolitan Museum of Art/Bequest of Rupert L.Joseph: 7b, 30t
StockXchange: 12b, 31r
Thinkstockphotos.com: 36-37c
Three Brothers Production: 47br
The Walters Art Museum, Baltimore: 7t

Every effort has been made to acknowledge correctly and contact the source and/or copyright holder of each picture and Carlton Books Limited apologises for any unintentional errors or omissions which will be corrected in future editions of this book.

THIS IS A CARLTON BOOK

Text, design and illustration © Carlton Books Limited 2012

Published in 2012 by Carlton Books Limited
An imprint of the Carlton Publishing Group
20 Mortimer Street, London W1T 3JW

10 9 8 7 6 5 4 3 2 1

A catalogue record for this book is available from the British Library.

ISBN: 978-1-78097-007-3

Printed in Dongguan, China